MW00574169

· 25 YEARS ·
F
BUILT to LAST

BOOKS BY JOHN MERWIN

Stillwater Trout *(ed.)*

McClane's Angling World
(ed., with A. J. McClane)

The Compleat McClane
(ed., with A. J. McClane)

John Merwin's Fly-Tying Guide

The Compleat Lee Wulff
(ed., with Lee Wulff)

The Compleat Schwiebert
(ed., with Ernest Schwiebert)

Salmon on a Fly
(ed., with Lee Wulff)

The Saltwater Tackle Box

The Freshwater Tackle Box

Streamer-Fly Fishing

The Battenkill

The New American Trout Fishing

Well-Cast Lines *(ed.)*

CONTRIBUTING AUTHOR:

The American Fly Tyer's Handbook

Waters Swift and Still

McClane's Game Fish of North America

Well-Cast Lines

THE FISHERMAN'S QUOTATION BOOK

COMPILED AND EDITED BY
JOHN MERWIN

FIRESIDE
Rockefeller Center
1230 Avenue of the Americas
New York, NY 10020

FIRESIDE and colophon are registered trademarks
of Simon & Schuster Inc.

Designed by Gretchen Achilles

Manufactured in the United States of America

10   9   8   7   6   5   4   3   2   1

Library of Congress Cataloging-in-Publication Data
Well-cast lines : the fisherman's quotation book / compiled and edited
    by John Merwin
        p.   cm.

    1. Fishing—Quotations, maxims, etc.   1. Merwin, John.
PN6084.F47W45   1995
799.1—dc20   95-34397
                                                                  CIP

ISBN 0-684-81151-0

A BOOK FOR EMILY,
WITH LOVE,
FROM YOUR DAD

*Some of the best fishing
is done not in water
but in print.*

SPARSE GREY HACKLE
(Alfred Miller, 1971)

Preface

Fishing makes strange bedfellows, to paraphrase an old chestnut about politics that I found courtesy of John Bartlett's *Familiar Quotations*, first published in 1855 and now in its sixteenth (1992) edition. As I compiled and edited this more modest collection relating to fish and fishing, I put the authors in last-name alphabetical order, hoping to make the book easy to use by making the authors easy to find. Arranged in that fashion, the bedfellows became odd, if not plain weird. And in that oddity, in those combinations that seemed at first peculiar, is a wonderful statement about fishing.

Here, for example, is Milford Stanley Poltroon, who wrote vitriolic angling satire in Montana during the 1970s (and whose real name was David Bascom), sandwiched between fishing commentaries by the Greek philosopher Plutarch and Alexander Pope, the eighteenth-century British classicist. Stirring the bedsheets further,

Oppian of ancient Rome is followed by O'Rourke of *Rolling Stone*. And Orvis and Ovid. But no Donder and Blitzen. This is a fishing book, after all.

It is an alphabetic accident that Frank Woolner's rough-and-ready wit kicks Izaak Walton's pastoral butt in these pages. But they both wrote well—if differently—about fishing, and so here they belong. Just as surely as Mary Orvis Marbury, the nineteenth-century American fly tier, follows Miss Manners and her proper prescription for eating fish. For women are part of fishing, and they belong here, too. Fishing, like Colt's revolver, is the great equalizer, but gently so; quiet fish and cool water instead of violence and fire, a place, as Herbert Hoover said, "to wash one's soul."

It is as an equalizer—and as a minor but common thread through three thousand years of civilization and literature—that fishing brings a diverse group to these pages. Some fish for metaphor—novelist John Cheever, for example—while others (the majority) are the hard core who fish for fish that are themselves not necessarily notable but that have prompted some notable words.

My selections are in some ways arbitrary. Fishermen are a contentious bunch, and I will hear a great deal, I know, about what I did—or didn't—include. I may have forgotten something, not thought of it, not known of it, or maybe your favorites just plain aren't mine. You can let me know. I have often been guilty—if guilt is the word—of all of those things. I looked for humor and found a great deal. I looked for wisdom and wit, and found much of that, too, while a search for tragedy and pathos brought only a little. Perhaps that speaks well of fishing.

I have avoided that which was racist—and there is some, especially before about 1930—or scatological or otherwise crude. And I made a serious attempt to include as many women as possible, both as authors and as subjects of particular quotes, while trying to avoid most of the many fishing jokes of which women are the tiresome butt. Many old chestnuts *are* here, such as John Donne's fifteenth-century poem involving "silver hooks." Is there a fisherman who doesn't know the first four lines by heart? Probably not, just as there are few fishermen who've read the whole thing, and for that reason I included that poem as well as a few other partly familiar things in their entirety.

John Bartlett was both a scholar and a fisherman of note. And like many fishermen, he collected things: decks of cards, fishing books (among many others), and quotations in general. He was well known in American literary circles by the time of the Civil War, and the poetic excerpt by James Russell Lowell that I've included was addressed by Lowell to his friend Bartlett in response to Bartlett's gift of a large fresh trout.

Like Bartlett in his nineteenth-century Massachusetts bookstore, I started collecting scrips and scraps of quotes twenty years ago when I first began editing a fishing magazine. The process continued through my years as director of the American Museum of Fly Fishing, where I lived daily with a two-thousand-volume angling library and browsed away my troubles when winter storms kept me from the Battenkill and the local bass ponds were frozen solid. I've used either primary or authoritative secondary sources for this book, and to that extent it may be a minor work of scholarship, although I make no such claim.

I would rather apply what Mark Twain said in his 1885 note that accompanied *Huckleberry Finn:*

> Persons attempting to find a motive in this narrative will be prosecuted; persons attempting to find a moral in it will be banished; persons attempting to find a plot in it will be shot.

This book is strictly for fun; yours and mine. For that reason I have not supplied references, explanations, notes, and citations in endless detail. We'll fish in these pages—at times thoughtfully, perhaps—and leave our worldly baggage behind.

JOHN MERWIN
Dorset, Vermont
September, 1994

Old Noah went a-fishing;
He sat upon the ark
And kept his hooks a-dangle
From daybreak on to dark.
His catch was pretty meager;
But every one affirms
He had no chance, because he
Had just a pair of worms.
ST. CLAIR ADAMS (C. 1915)

Men first appeared as fishes. When they were able to help themselves they took to the land.
ANAXIMANDER (C. 580 B.C.)

If you swear, you will catch no fish.
ANON. (ENGLISH PROVERB, C. 1600)

You're a salmon in Dracut but a pollack in Boston!
ANON. (1844)

When the wind is in the east,
Then the fishes bite the least;
When the wind is in the west,
Then the fishes bite the best;
When the wind is in the north,
Then the fishes do come forth;
When the wind is in the south,
It blows the bait in the fish's mouth.
ANON. (C. 1850)

Fish or cut bait.
ANON. (20TH-CENTURY AMERICANISM)

If you wish to be happy for an hour, get intoxicated.
If you wish to be happy for three days, get married.
If you wish to be happy for eight days, kill your pig and eat it.
If you wish to be happy forever, learn to fish.
ANON. (CHINESE PROVERB)

It is not a fish until it is on the bank.
ANON. (IRISH PROVERB)

Bragging may not bring happiness, but no man having caught a large fish goes home through an alley.
ANON.

They say that the Egyptians are clever in that they rank the eel equal to a god, but in reality it is held in esteem and value far higher than gods, for *them* we can propitiate with a prayer or two, while to get even a smell of an eel at Athens we may have to spend twelve drachmae or more!
ANTIPHANES (C. 325 B.C.)

A fiddler on a fish through waves advanced,
He twang'd the catgut, and the dolphins danced.
ARION (C. 600 B.C.)

Some people dwelling near the sea affirm that of all living creatures the fish is the quickest of hearing.
ARISTOTLE (C. 340 B.C.)

The gods do not subtract from the allotted span of men's lives the hours spent in fishing.
ASSYRIAN TABLET (2000 B.C.)

A rising fish. Sunset and scenery are at once forgotten. We must get that beggar!
GEORGE ASTON (1926)

Most anglers spend their lives in making rules for trout, and trout spend theirs in breaking them.
GEORGE ASTON (1926)

Angling . . . has taught me about art, as art has led to interesting theories and experiments in angling. Thinking and fishing go well together somehow.

JOHN ATHERTON (1951)

The cat-fish is a voracious creature, not at all nice in feeding, but one who, like the vulture, contents himself with carrion when nothing better can be had.

JOHN JAMES AUDUBON (1835)

"What a delightful thing is fishing!" have I more than once heard some knowing angler exclaim, who, with "the patience of Job," stands or slowly moves along some rivulet twenty feet wide, and three or four feet deep, with a sham fly to allure a trout, which, when at length caught, weighs half a pound.

Reader, I never had such patience. Although I have waited ten years and yet see only three-fourths of the *Birds of America* engraved, although some of the drawings of that work were patiently made so long ago as 1805, and although I have to wait with patience two years more before I see the end of it, I could never hold a line or a rod for many minutes, unless I had—not a "nibble," but a hearty bite, and could throw the fish at once over my head on the ground.

No, no—if I fish for trout, I must soon give up, or catch, as I have done in Pennsylvania's Lehigh, or the streams of Maine, fifty or more in a couple of hours.

JOHN JAMES AUDUBON (1835)

Nor let the Muse, in her award of fame,
Illustrious perch, unnoticed pass thy claim;
Prince of the prickly cohort, bred in lakes
To feast our boards, what sapid boneless flakes
Thy solid flesh supplies! Though river-fed,
No daintier fish in ocean's pastures bred
Swims thy compeer; scarce mullet may compete
With thee for fiber firm and flavor sweet.

AUSONIUS (C. 385)

Don't ye talk to me of work!
    I'm jest goin' fishin'
Where the speckled beauties lurk,
    'Round the pools a-swishin'
Ne'er a thought have I of care,

Settin' on a green bank there,
Drinkin' in the soft June air,
Void of all ambition!
JOHN KENDRICK BANGS
(C. 1910)

The great fish eat the small.
ALEXANDER BARCLAY (1509)

Suckers are trash fish, an insult to divinity. They have chubby, humanoid lips and appear to be begging for cigars.
BILL BARICH (1981)

As inward love breeds outward talk,
The hound some praise, and some the hawk,
Some, better pleas'd with private sport,
Use tennis, some a mistress court:
But these delights I neither wish,
Nor envy, while I freely fish.
WILLIAM BARRE (C. 1640)

Has it ever struck you that trouts bite best on the Sabbath? God's critters tempting decent men.

JAMES BARRIE (1891)

Remember when President Bush was taking his biweekly vacation up in Kenneth E. Bunkport IV, Maine, and he failed to catch any fish, day after day, until it became a national news story of greater urgency than Lebanon, and the whole federal government apparatus seemed to shudder to a halt while the Leader of the Free World . . . was off somewhere trying to outwit an organism with a brain the size of a hydrogen atom?

DAVE BARRY (1991)

Fishing, if I a fisher may protest,
Of Pleasures is the sweetest, of sports the best,
Of exercises the most excellent,
Of recreations the most innocent,
But now the sport is marred, and wott ye why?
Fishes decrease, and fishers multiply.

THOMAS BASTARD (1598)

I am *not* a lady fly fisher; I am a fly fisherman.
  LADY BEAVERKILL (MRS. LOUISE MILLER, C. 1965)

If I was a deacon, I wouldn't let a fish's tail whisk the whole Catechism out of my head.
  HENRY WARD BEECHER (1868)

And when he struck his first cod, and felt the fish take the hook, a kind of big slow smile went over his features, and he said, "Gentlemen, this is solid comfort."
  STEPHEN VINCENT BENÉT (1932)

The streams alone offer relief that is complete. When he feels the rush of cold water against his waders and pits his skill against the natural instincts and wariness of the trout everything else is lost in the sheer joy of the moment.
  RAY BERGMAN (1938)

Although my enthusiasm for trout fishing and my fondness for the dry fly . . . are as long standing as my bass experience, I esteem the bass and am always heart-stricken by the blasphemy against them so often expressed by rabid trout fishermen.

RAY BERGMAN (1942)

And if the angler catches the fish with difficulty, then there is no man merrier than he is in his spirits.

JULIANA BERNERS (1450)

And for the principal point of angling, always keep yourself away from the water and from the sight of the fish—far back on the land or else behind a bush or a tree—so that the fish may not see you. For if he does, he will not bite.

JULIANA BERNERS (1450)

You cannot bring a hook into a fish's mouth unless there is food on it that pleases him.

JULIANA BERNERS (1450)

You must not be too greedy in catching your said game [fish], as in taking too much at one time. . . . That could easily be the occasion of destroying your own sport and other men's also.

JULIANA BERNERS (1450)

I doubt not, that the use of the fly among the mountains, or wherever the trout are found, is nearly as old as the first knowledge that trout were delicate eating.

GEORGE WASHINGTON BETHUNE (1847)

This island [England] is made mainly of coal and surrounded by fish. Only an organizing genius could produce a shortage of coal and fish at the same time.

ANEURIN BEVAN (1945)

Fishing seems like being in the arms of a beautiful mother, the gracious solitary event when you find out that you are alone in the world, but it is all right because your mother is there, too. It is not really the kind of thing you learn while fishing, but rather only in retrospect as you grow older and have only rare opportunities to fish.

JANNA BIALEK (1991)

If I were a jolly archbishop,
On Fridays I'd eat all the fish up—
Salmon and flounders and smelts;
On other days everything else.

AMBROSE BIERCE (1906)

BAIT, n. A preparation that renders the hook more palatable. The best kind is beauty.

AMBROSE BIERCE (1906)

SEINE, n. A kind of net for effecting an involuntary change of environment. For fish it is made strong and coarse, but women are more easily taken with a singularly delicate fabric weighted with small, cut stones.

AMBROSE BIERCE (1906)

But what is the test of a river? "The power to drown a man," replies the river darkly.

R. D. BLACKMORE (1895)

The unique ardor of the trout fisherman is best complimented by blaming failure, not on his own ineptness, but on the devastating cunning of his wily antagonist.

HAROLD BLAISDELL (1969)

I chose my cast, a march-brown and a dun,
And ran down to the river, chasing hope.

WILFRID S. BLUNT (1889)

PECOS BILL GOES FISHING

During Pecos Bill's time there was a lot of people that didn't believe there was any sech animal as the whiffle-pooffle livin' in the bottom of the lakes. Bill said he knowed there was, and he'd show 'em. So he studied and studied, and finally he found a way to capture the critters. First he gits together a rowboat, a long post-hole auger, and a can of oil. Then he hunts up the funniest story-teller he can find and takes him along and sets out.

He rows out on to the lake where the water's deep; then he takes the post-hole auger and bores a hole clean down to the bottom so as the whiffle-pooffle can come up to the top. Then he has the story-teller tell the funniest stories he can think of. . . .

Purty soon the whiffle-pooffle gits interested and pricks up his ears. Then Bill tells the story-teller to git funnier. Then purty soon the whiffle-pooffle is so amused that he comes up through the hole and sticks out his head. Bill tells the man to keep on gittin' funnier and funnier till the whiffle-pooffle comes clean out of the water. Then Bill begins to ply the oars, very gentle-like at first. The whiffle-pooffle is so interested and amused that he jest naturally can't help but foller the story-teller, who all the time is gittin' funnier and funnier. Bill rows faster and faster, all the time makin' straight for the bank.

Jest before he gits there, when he is rowin' as fast as he can, he pours the oil out on the water and cuts sharply to the left. By that time the whiffle-pooffle has got up so much speed on the slick water that he can't stop, and he just naturally slides right out on the bank. Then Pecos Bill lands on him . . .

MOADY BOATRIGHT (1934)

She liked men, liked being with them, but not on a stream. That was one place where males were too apt to be solicitous and distracting.

PAUL BONNER (1954)

If you ever wondered why fishing is probably the most popular sport in this country, watch that boy beside the brook and you will learn. If you are really perceptive you will. For he already knows that fishing is only one part fish.

HAL BORLAND (1954)

Fish? Oh, yes, one must have a reason and the day must have a purpose. But it's the fishing, really, the dawn and the morning and the day, and man's knowing that it's still there, still real.

HAL BORLAND (1955)

If you were to make little fishes talk, they would talk like whales.

JAMES BOSWELL (1791)

Now I am . . . like anyone with a strong preference for the fly rod, totally indifferent to how large a fish I catch by comparison with other fishermen. So when a fifteen-year-old called Fred, fishing deep in midsummer with a hideous plastic worm, caught a four-and-a-half pounder . . . I naturally felt no resentment beyond wanting to break the kid's thumbs.

VANCE BOURJAILY (1981)

The old drunk told me about trout fishing. When he could talk, he had a way of describing trout as if they were precious and intelligent metal.

Silver is not a good adjective to describe what I felt when he told me about trout fishing.

I'd like to get it right.

Maybe trout steel. Steel made from trout. The clear snow-filled river acting as foundry and heat.

RICHARD BRAUTIGAN (1967)

Used trout stream for sale. Must be seen to be appreciated.

RICHARD BRAUTIGAN (1967)

Or along the shallow brooke,
Angling with a baited hooke:
See the fishes leape and play
In a blessed Sunny day.
NICHOLAS BRETON (1604)

A beautiful stream to one man is just so much water in which he may possibly catch so many trout.
ARTHUR BRISBANE (C. 1900)

Fish say, they have their Stream and Pond;
But is there anything beyond?
RUPERT BROOKE (1915)

Oh! never fly conceals a hook,
Fish say, in the Eternal Brook,
But more than mundane weeds are there,
And mud; celestially fair;
Fat caterpillars drift around,
And Paradisal grubs are found;

> Unfading moths, immortal flies,
> And the worm that never dies.
> And in that Heaven of all their wish,
> There shall be no more land, say fish.
> *RUPERT BROOKE (1915)*

The sight of a bonefish tail waving slowly above the surface of the shallow water where he customarily feeds does all kinds of things to you. You shiver and shake and tingle all over and your mouth goes dry. It is one of the great moments of all fishing experience.

JOE BROOKS (1950)

Of the many species of fish, each has its own special appeal, but none has the universal charisma of the trout . . . of all fish, the trout demands the most of the angler . . . and gives the most in return.

JOE BROOKS (1972)

PAUL BUNYAN'S NATURAL HISTORY OF FISH

COUGAR FISH: This savage fish, armed with sharp claws, lived in the Big Onion River. It was the cause of the disappearance and death of many river drivers, whom it clawed off the logs and beneath the water. Paul Bunyan offered a big reward for their capture and extermination, but the fish heard of it and stayed away. None were taken.

GIDDY FISH: They were small and very elastic, like India rubber. They were caught through holes in the ice during the winter. The method pursued was to hit one on the head with a paddle. This fish would bounce up and down. Taking the cue from him the other fish would bounce also. Presently all would bounce themselves out of the water onto the ice. There they were easily gathered up.

GOOFANG: This curious fish always swam backward instead of forward. This was to keep the water out of its eyes. It was described as "about the size of a sunfish, only larger."

LOG GAR: These big fish had a snout so well armed with large saw teeth that they could saw right through a log to get at a juicy lumberjack. Once in the water they made mince meat of him.

UPLAND TROUT: These very adroit fish built their nests in trees and were very difficult to take. They flew well but never entered the water. They were fine pan fish. Tenderfeet were sent out into the woods to catch them.

WHIRLIGIG FISH: Related to the Giddy Fish. They always swam in circles. They were taken in the winter months through holes in the ice, like their relatives. The loggers smeared the edges of the holes with ham or bacon rind. Smelling this the fish would swim around the rims of the holes, faster and faster, until they whirled themselves out on the ice. Thousands were thus taken.

C. E. BROWN (1935)

The scientific and graceful art of throwing the artificial fly is a beautiful accomplishment, but not so difficult as is generally imagined.

JOHN BROWN (1849)

The charm of fishing is that it is the pursuit of what is elusive but attainable, a perpetual series of occasions for hope.

JOHN BUCHAN (1915)

You see the way the Fisherman doth take
To catch the Fish; what Engins doth he make?
Behold how he ingageth all his wits,
Also his Snares, Lines, Angles, Hooks, and Nets.
Yet fish there be, that neither Hook, nor Line,
Nor Snare, nor Net, nor Engin can make thine;
They must be grop't for, and be tickled too,
Or they will not be catch't, whate'er you do.
JOHN BUNYAN (1678)

I came from a race of fishers, trout streams gurgled about the roots
of my family tree.
JOHN BURROUGHS (1884)

When you bait your hook with your heart, the fish always bite!
JOHN BURROUGHS (C. 1885)

A certain quality of youth is indispensable to the successful angler,
a certain unworldliness and readiness to invest yourself in an enter-
prise that doesn't pay in the current coin.
JOHN BURROUGHS (C. 1885)

"Lyin' is lyin', be it about fish or money, and is forbid by Scripter. . . . Billy Matison's got to give up fish-lyin', or he won't never get into the kingdom."

ELLIS PARKER BUTLER (1899)

Whatever Izaak Walton sings or says:
The quaint, old, cruel coxcomb, in his gullet
Should have a hook, and a small trout to pull it.

LORD BYRON (1823)

The sea hath fish for every man.

WILLIAM CAMDEN (1605)

The near sound of rivers, like the far sound of geese in flight, plays on one's consciousness without resolution.

CHRISTOPHER CAMUTO (1990)

When you visit strange waters go alone. . . . Play the game out with the stream! Go to it completely handicapped by all your ignorance. Then all you learn will be your very own.

    R. SINCLAIR CARR (1936)

How cheerfully he seems to grin,
How neatly spreads his claws,
And welcomes little fishes in
With gently smiling jaws!
    LEWIS CARROLL (1865)

With nary one fish to show for his day with rod and reel, an amateur fisherman stopped at a market on his way home and thoughtfully bought a dozen trout. He then ordered the fish man to throw them to him one at a time. "When I tell my wife," he explained to the mystified fish man, "that I catch fish—*I catch them!*"

    BENNETT CERF (1965)

There is no taking trout with dry breeches.

    CERVANTES (1615)

Fishing at its most rudimentary level is essentially solitary. Not only that, but its components, outside the particular baggage one brings to it, are entirely trustworthy. I mean, what creek ever teased you about your pimples; what breeze ever ridiculed you in front of your friends?

RUSSELL CHATHAM (1978)

There's joy in the chase, over hedge and ditch flying;
'Tis pleasant to bring down the grouse on the fell;
The partridge to bag, through the low stubble trying;
The pheasant to shoot as he flies through the dell.
But what are such joys to the pleasures of straying
By the side of a stream, a long line throwing free,
The salmon and trout with a neat fly betraying?
Fit your rods, and away to the fishing with me!

WILLIAM CHATTO (1834)

He learned to cast with a fly rod, feeling that, cast by cast, he might work his way into the terrain of his father's affection and esteem, but his father had never found time to admire him.

JOHN CHEEVER (1978)

Even a little kid wouldn't try to catch fish without a sinker. Of course, somebody with no sense might go fishing without a sinker. No rules for fools.
ANTON CHEKHOV (1895)

We are waiting for the long-promised invasion. So are the fishes.
WINSTON CHURCHILL (1940)

The best fish swim near the bottom.
JOHN CLARKE (1639)

It must, of course, be admitted, that large stories of fishing adventure are sometimes told by fishermen—and why should this not be so? Beyond all question there is no sphere of human activity so full of strange and wonderful incidents as theirs.
GROVER CLEVELAND (1901)

The strike is a gift, a gift the barracuda keeps for its fishermen and always gives with grace. Even though the fish has been seen, even though the impending contact has been announced by the creature itself, the meeting has the jolt of a slap on the shins with a two-by-four, the shock of a kick in the groin.

WHAM!

JOHN COLE (1989)

"I don't know what's going to become of you, John." He shook his head, his eyes angry, his fist in knots. "The only two things you care about are fishing and fucking. Nothing else means a damn thing to you."

"Well, at least you got the order right," I said.

JOHN COLE (1989)

As there will never be enough fishing books in the world, I offer no apology for adding this one to the groaning shelves of angling literature.

EUGENE CONNETT (1933)

And when you discover that you have tied a killing fly with your own hands, and have made a reluctant trout take it, you will then know the fullness of an intelligent angler's pleasure.

EUGENE CONNETT (1961)

At the altar, I little realized I was pledged to love, honor, and obey three outboard motors, the ways of the river, the whims of the tide, and the wiles of the fish, as well as Bill, the man of my choice.

BEATRICE COOK (1949)

The world has no better fish than the bass of Otsego [a lake whitefish]; it unites the richness of the shad to the firmness of the salmon.

JAMES FENIMORE COOPER (1823)

For the length of your rod you are always to be governed by the breadth of the river you shall choose to angle at; and for a trout river, one of five or six yards long is commonly enough, and longer it ought not to be, if you intend to fish at ease, and of otherwise, where lies the sport?

CHARLES COTTON (1676)

. . . to fish fine and far off is the first and principal rule for trout angling.

CHARLES COTTON (1676)

What a shame and pity is then, that such a river should be destroyed by the basest sort of people.

CHARLES COTTON (1676)

A RECIPE FOR TROUT

Take your trout, wash, and dry him with a clean napkin; then open him, and having taken out his guts, and all the blood, wipe him very clean within, but wash him not, and give him three scotches with a knife to the bone on one side only. After which take a clean kettle, and put in as much hard, stale beer (but it must not be dead) vinegar, and a little white wine, and water, as will cover the fish you intend to boil; then throw into the liquor a good quantity of salt, the rind of a lemon, a handful of sliced horse-radish root, with a handsome little faggot of rosemary, thyme, and winter-savory. Then set your kettle upon a quick fire of wood, and let your liquor boil up to the height before you put in your fish, and then, if there be many, put them in one by one, that they may not so cool the liquor as to make it fall; and whilst your fish is boiling, beat up the butter for your sauce with a ladleful or two of the liquor it is boiling in, and being boiled enough, immediately pour the liquor from the fish, and being laid in a dish, pour your butter upon it, and strewing it plentifully over with shaved horse-radish, and a little pounded ginger, garnish your sides of your dish, and the fish itself with a sliced lemon, or two, and serve it up.

CHARLES COTTON (1676)

Man is separated from the shark by an abyss of time. The fish still lives in the late Mesozoic, when the rocks were made; it has changed but little in perhaps three hundred million years. Across the gulf of ages, which evolved other marine creatures, the relentless, indestructible shark has come without need of evolution, the oldest killer, armed for the fray of existence in the beginning.

JACQUES COUSTEAU (1954)

And what would become of the lawyers and trout—
Trout, trout, and the devil all out,
If clients, like hoppers, warn't lyin' about—
Whack-fal-larity—whack-fal-larity—
And it warn't for wanitee? [vanity]

DAVID CROSS (1880)

THREE FISH TALES

It seems that Bill was fishing without any success when by chance he looked in the weeds beside him and there was a small garter snake with a frog halfway in his mouth. . . . He grabbed the snake by the neck and pulled the frog out and slipped it on his hook. Looking down, he thought the snake seemed very quiet and depressed. Being a square shooter, Bill thought he should give the snake something in return for the frog, so he yanked out his ever-ready flask and poured a wee drop of its contents down the snake's throat. Sometime later . . . Bill felt something poking him on the leg. Looking down, he saw the snake with a happy expression in his eyes and, sure enough, another small frog just about the right size for those large Cranberry [Lake] trout.

. . .

Dick . . . was fishing at the state camp on the east branch of the Neversink, April 24, 1938, using a bucktail as a lure. He took an eighteen-inch native trout which had a seven-inch and two five-inch trout in its stomach—nearly ate its length in fish. I told this incident to Tony, who allowed that was nothing as he had eaten many times his own length in spaghetti at one sitting.

. . .

A brother angler and author whom most of us know either person-
ally or through his writing was fishing the Beaverkill near Cook's
Falls one day, and there were several boys watching him from up
on the bridge. After he had landed a nice trout, one of the boys
called down, "Hey mister, what are you getting them on?"

"Cowdung [a wet-fly pattern]," was the brief reply.

After a bit of silence, the young rascal called down, "Hey,
mister, did you ever try horse manure?"

REUBEN CROSS (1940)

The art of fishing can be the art of catching an idea with all the
energy and sophistication we can cast into the deepest mind pool.

JACK CURTIS (1978)

THE SKELETON ANGLER

When the old clock in yon grey tower
Proclaims the deep, still midnight hour,
And ominous birds are on the wing,
I rise from the realms of the bony king.
My bonny elm coffin I shoulder and take
To fish in the blood-red phantom lake,

Where many a brace of spectral trout
For ever frisk, dart, and frolic about;
Then the hyena's ravening voice
Gladdens and makes my heart rejoice.
The glow-worm and the death's-head moth
Are killing baits on the crimson froth.
For work-bench I've the sculptured tomb
Where tackle I form by the silent moon;
Of churchyard yew my rods I make;
Worms from the putrid corpse I take;
Lines I plait from the golden hair
Plucked from the head of a damsel fair;
Floats of the mournful cypress tree
I carve while the night-winds whistle free;
My plummets are moulded of coffin lead;
For paste I seize the parish bread;
The screech-owl's or the raven's wing
For making flies are just the thing.
Should thunder roll, from the barren shore
I bob for eels in the crimson gore;
A human skull is my live-bait can;
My ground-bait the crumbling bones of man;
My lusty old coffin for a punt I take
To angle by night in the phantom lake.

While Dante's winged demons are hovering o'er
The skeleton trout of the crimson gore,
To the blood-red phantom lake I go,
While vampire bats flit to and fro.

SCENE THE SECOND (SUNRISE)

The owl is at roost in his ivy'd bower,
The bat hangs up in the old church tower,
The raven's head is beneath his wing,
The skeleton sleeps with the bony king,
The fierce hyena has left the grave
To seek repose in his darksome cave.
The author of this piscatorial treat
Is the far-famed E. Davis, of King William Street;
Twenty-one is the number o'erlooking the Strand;
His prices are lowest of all in the land.

E. DAVIS (C. 1870)

Ann, Ann!
Come quick as you can!
There's a fish that *talks*
In the frying-pan.

WALTER DE LA MARE (1913)

The death of the fish is both the cause for impersonality in the fisherman and of profound regret . . . no one can have seen the dolphin come to air without a feeling of profound sorrow and loss. Here is this quivering splinter of nature turned by sullen and perverse magic from being a combination of incandescent greens and yellows into a mottled and mediocre neutral tone: yes, the thing has been done, and something taken away.

JAMES DICKEY (1978)

If the old boy [Izaak Walton] occasionally stretched the truth, it strikes me that it makes him an even more appropriate father figure for a cult whose members are often given to hyperbole.

ROBERT DIENDORFER (1977)

Fish! They manage to be so water-colored. Theirs is not the color of the bottom but the color of the light itself, the light dissolved like a powder in the water. They disappear and reappear as if by spontaneous generation: sleight of fish.

ANNIE DILLARD (1974)

It seems impossible to exaggerate the fishing possibilities of the west coast of Florida. With a fly rod the number of fish which may be caught is purely a question of physical endurance.

A. W. DIMOCK (1890)

THE BAIT

Come live with me, and be my love,
And we will some new pleasures prove
Of golden sands, and crystal brooks,
With silken lines and silver hooks.

There will the river whisp'ring run,
Warm'd by thy eyes more than the Sun;
And there th' enamour'd fish will stay,
Begging themselves they may betray.

When thou wilt swim in that live bath,
Each fish, which every channel hath,
Most am'rously to thee will swim,
Gladder to catch thee, than thou him.

If thou, to be so seen, be'st loth,
By Sun, or Moon, thou dark'nest both,
And if myself have leave to see,
I need not their light, having thee.

Let others freeze with angling reeds,
And cut their legs, with shells and weeds,
Or treach'rously poor fish beset,
With strangling snare, or windowy net:

Let coarse bold hands, from slimy nest,
The bedded fish in banks out-wrest;
Let curious traitors, sleeve-silk flies,
Bewitch poor fishes' wand'ring eyes.

For thee, thou need'st no such deceit,
For thou thyself, art thine own bait;
That fish, that is not catch'd thereby,
Alas! is wiser far than I.

JOHN DONNE (C. 1598)

Of all the world's enjoyments
That ever valued were,
There's none of our employments
With fishing can compare.
THOMAS D'URFEY (1719)

Pike—great northern. A fish that packs brass knuckles on his jaws
and a blackjack in his tail.
BEN EAST (1947)

Fly fishers fail in preparing their bait so as to make it alluring in
the right quarter, for want of a due acquaintance with the subjectivity of fishes.
GEORGE ELIOT (MARY ANN EVANS, 1860)

If I had been a bottle baby, I would have fished in my formula.
BOB ELLIOT (1950)

Beauty without grace is the hook without the bait.
RALPH WALDO EMERSON (1860)

The fishing was so good, I thought I was there yesterday.
DAVE ENGERBRETSON (1994)

The sea is terrible or benign, but always infinite, and the surf fisherman feels this in the marrow of his bones.
VLAD EVANOFF (C. 1972)

Every man has a fish in his life that haunts him.
NEGLEY FARSON (1942)

I'm not saying that all fly fishing, yes, even bait-casting, is not a fine art . . . , but I do think that there are far too many people who are satisfied to accumulate tackle and terminology, rather than to fish.
NEGLEY FARSON (1942)

I never lost a *little* fish—yes, I am free to say
It always was the biggest fish I caught that got away.
EUGENE FIELD (1889)

SIMPSON: "Have you seen any American books on angling,
                    Fisher?"

FISHER: "No, I do not think there are any published. Brother
                    Jonathan is not yet sufficiently civilized to produce
                    anything original on the gentle art."
       PAUL FISHER (BRITISH, 1835)

It should be remembered that the way small trout rise to artificials
is no criterion, and dry flies should not be judged by their ability
to catch the little fellows that do not know what it is all about.
       ART FLICK (1969)

The woods are made for the hunters of dreams,
The brooks for the fishers of song.
       SAM FOSS (C. 1900)

You can always tell a fisherman, but you can't tell him much.
       COREY FORD (C. 1940)

Constituation of the Lower Forty:

ARTICKLE ONE: RULES.
They ain't no rules.

ARTICKLE TWO: PRESIDENT.
Everybody's President.

ARTICKLE THREE: MEMBERSHIP.
If ennybody else wants to join this club, go ahead, but don't
bother us about it. We've went fishing.
COREY FORD (1953)

A friend of mine, an ardent purist, was challenged once by a
golfing acquaintance as he turned loose a large trout he had just
netted. "Why go to all that trouble to catch a fish," the exasperated
golfer demanded, "if you don't want to eat it?"

"Do you eat golf balls?" my friend inquired.
COREY FORD (1958)

There is not a pleasanter summer day's amusement than a merry cruise after the Blue-Fish, no pleasanter close to it than the clam-bake, the chowder, and the broiled Blue-Fish, lubricated with champagne.

FRANK FORRESTER (1851)

Bait casting, which many people prefer to call plugging, is a relatively new sport, and it is the only phase of angling that is as American as baseball, ice-cream cones, and Pike's Peak.

CHARLES K. FOX (1950)

The climax in the poem of trouting is the spring of the split bamboo.

LEWIS FRANCE (1884)

Death is a Fisherman, the world we see
His Fish-pond is, and we the Fishes be.
His Net some general Sickness; howe'er he
Is not so kind as other Fishers be,
For if they take one of the smaller Fry,

They throw him in again, he shall not die;
But Death is sure to kill all he can get,
And all is fish with him that comes to Net.
BENJAMIN FRANKLIN (1733)

The end of fishing is not angling, but catching.
THOMAS FULLER (1732)

It is a silly fish that is caught twice with the same bait.
THOMAS FULLER (1732)

Fishermen are characters. They have more idiosyncrasies than a mother alligator has babies.
R. V. GADABOUT GADDIS (1967)

Fish are strange creatures. They're even more unpredictable than women—and that's going some.
R. V. GADABOUT GADDIS (1967)

When if an insect fall (his certain guide)
He gently takes him from the whirling tide;
Examines well his form with curious eyes,
His gaudy vest, his wings, his horns and size,
Then round his hook the chosen fur he winds,
And on the back a speckled feather binds,
So just the colours shine thro' ev'ry part,
That nature seems to live again in art.
JOHN GAY (1720)

Around the steel no tortur'd worm shall twine,
No blood of living insect stain my line;
Let me, less cruel, cast feather'd hook,
With pliant rod athwart the pebbled brook,
Silent along the mazy margin stray,
And with fur-wrought fly delude the prey.
JOHN GAY (1720)

Fish die belly-up and rise to the surface; it is their way of falling.
ANDRÉ GIDE (1930)

Such is fly fishing: almost anything that happens can be a triumph when the proper logic is applied.

JOHN GIERACH (1986)

Here's a pretty kettle of fish!

WILLIAM GILBERT (1882)

If all men are equal, then who am I to hold out for class distinctions between fish?

ARNOLD GINGRICH (1959)

THE SEA ANGLER

There was a gentle angler who was angling in the sea,
With heart as cool as only heart, untaught of love, can be;
When suddenly the waters rushed, and swelled, and up there
    sprung
A humid maid of beauty's mould—and thus to him she sung:

"Why dost thou strive so artfully to lure my brood away,
And leave them then to die beneath the sun's all-scorching ray?
Couldst thou but tell how happy are the fish that swim below,
Thou wouldst with me, and taste of joy which earth can never
    know. . . ."

The water rushed, the water swelled, and touched his naked feet,
And fancy whispered to his heart it was a love-pledge sweet:
She sung another siren lay, more 'wiching than before,
Half-pulled—half plunging—down he sunk, and ne'er was heard
    of more.
    JOHANN WOLFGANG VON GOETHE (C. 1780)

Anglers are too apt to pin their faith to two or three favorite flies,
and to imagine that if the trout should not rise at these, they will
not take at all.
    THEODORE GORDON (1903)

The enormous increase in the number of anglers in recent years
has made it necessary that all true sportsmen should consider the
interests of others as well as their own.
    THEODORE GORDON (1903)

I am surprised that more ladies do not take an interest in fly-fishing. It is well within their powers, and those accustomed to exercise soon become enthusiastic.

THEODORE GORDON (1903)

When we have good luck we come home early; otherwise we stay late and fight it out. How often we are defeated! Everything goes against us and we struggle in vain to conquer adverse conditions, but if we do win out, how pleased we are. We really believe that we can fish.

THEODORE GORDON (1906)

A visit to a first-class fishing-tackle shop is more interesting than an afternoon at the circus.

THEODORE GORDON (1906)

Fly making gives us a new sense almost. We are constantly on the lookout, and view everything with an added interest. Possibly we may turn it into a bug of some kind.

THEODORE GORDON (1907)

The great charm of fly-fishing is that we are always learning; no matter how long we have been at it, we are constantly making some fresh discovery, picking up some new wrinkle. If we become conceited through great success, some day the trout will take us down a peg.

THEODORE GORDON (1907)

I am fond of all sorts of fishing, in fresh or salt water, in the interior of the country, or on the coast, but trout angling takes a grip on the imagination. It is more of a mental recreation than other methods.

THEODORE GORDON (1908)

Once an angler, always a fisherman. If we cannot have the best, we will take the least, and fish for minnows if nothing better is to be had.

THEODORE GORDON (1912)

It is just as well to remember that angling is only a recreation, not a profession. We usually find that men of the greatest experience are the most liberal and least dogmatic . . . it is often the man of limited experience who is most confident.

THEODORE GORDON (1914)

They may the better fish in the waters when it is troubled.

RICHARD GRAFTON (1569)

I gave the fish back to the river, or gave it back to them: shapely, fork-tailed, bright silver creatures with thin dark parallel striping along their sides, gaping rhythmically from the struggle's exhaustion as they eased backward from my hand in the slow shallows.

JOHN GRAVES (1981)

A fisherman is a lazy bad boy grown up. . . . He is dirty and disobedient, he plays hooky and won't work. Then when he gets to be a man, all he does is trudge off to Joe's Run or Licking Creek with a long fishing pole over his shoulder.

ZANE GREY (1924)

I've had my share of fishing joy,
    I've fished with patent bait,
With chub and minnow, but the boy
    Is lord of sport's estate.
And no such pleasure comes to man
    So rare as when he took
A worm from a tomato can
    And slipped it on a hook.
EDGAR GUEST (C. 1935)

Dry-fly fishing is more a woman's than a man's game. What are the requirements? Dexterity and good coordination, fast and well-controlled reflexes, and light and sensitive touch, keen eyesight, and close concentration. Any industrial personnel man will assure you that women are greatly superior to men in these respects.
SPARSE GREY HACKLE (ALFRED MILLER, 1971)

This is night fishing . . . a gorgeous gambling game in which one stakes the certainty of long hours of faceless fumbling, nerve-racking starts, frights, falls, and fishless baskets against the off chance of hooking into . . . a fish as long and heavy as a railroad tie and as unmanageable as a runaway submarine.

SPARSE GREY HACKLE (ALFRED MILLER, 1971)

Fish are, of course, indispensable to the angler. They give him an excuse for fishing and justify the flyrod without which he would be a mere vagrant.

SPARSE GREY HACKLE (ALFRED MILLER, 1972)

I want fish from fishing, but I want a great deal more than that, and getting it is not always dependent upon catching fish.

RODERICK HAIG-BROWN (1946)

If one has to die, I should think November would be the month for it. It is a gray stormy month; the salmon are dying, and the year is done. . . . When the time comes, if I know what it's all about, I suppose I shall think, among other things, of the fish I haven't caught and the places I haven't fished.

RODERICK HAIG-BROWN (1946)

It is just possible that nice guys don't catch the most fish. But they find far more pleasure in those they do get.

RODERICK HAIG-BROWN (1960)

As the winds stir and drift the dying leaves, so the waters drift and stir the dying salmon against the gray-brown gravels of the stream beds. But under those gravels life is strong and secret and protected in the buried eggs, the real life of the race. . . . In spring life will burst from the gravel as it bursts again from the trees, into the massive yield of the new cycle. Death is seldom more fleeting or more fertile than this.

RODERICK HAIG-BROWN (1964)

This is what fishing is all about. Not just repeating over and over the things one knows can be done. Not just catching and killing. . . . It is in developing and refining knowledge of the fish themselves and, with this understanding, finding ways of taking them that show them at their best.

RODERICK HAIG-BROWN (1971)

It is self-evident that no fish which inhabit foul or sluggish waters can be "game fish.". . . They may flash with tinsel and tawdry attire; they may strike with the brute force of a blacksmith, or exhibit the dexterity of a prizefighter, but their low breeding and vulgar quality cannot be mistaken.

CHARLES HALLOCK (1873)

"Heyo, Brer Rabbit! Who you wizzitin' down dar?"

"Who? Me? Oh, I'm des a fishin', Brer Fox," sez Brer Rabbit, sezee. "I des say ter myse'f dat I'd sorter sprize you all wid a mess er fishes fer dinner, en so here I is, en dar's de fishes. I'm a fishin' fer suckers, Brer Fox," sez Brer Rabbit, sezee.

JOEL CHANDLER HARRIS (1880)

Fishing makes us less the hostages to the horrors of making a living.

JIM HARRISON (1978)

The best bet for white shark is an aborigine mongoloid or a whole kangaroo. If properly hooked, the kangaroo will swim for hours in ever-decreasing circles. Sharks think of them as furry space cookies.

JIM HARRISON (1978)

The true force behind ice fishing is that it is better than no fishing at all. In extremis, an addictive fisherman will shoot carp with a bow and arrow, set up trotlines for carp and suckers, spear dogfish on Pig Trotter Creek, chum nurse sharks within rifle range. He will surround the crudest equipment with a mystique and will maintain to the uninitiated that there's no sport quite like fishing rainbows with bobber and marshmallows.

JIM HARRISON (1978)

There is nothing which in a moment makes a tired, despondent, perhaps hopeless man suddenly become alert and keen as the hooking of a big fish.

GILFRID HARTLEY (C. 1920)

> King of the brook,
>   No fisher's hook
> Fills me with dread of the sweaty cook;
>   But here I lie,
>   And laugh, as they try;
> Shall I bite at their bait? no, no, not I!
>   *W. P. HAWES (1842)*

About ninety in a hundred fancy themselves anglers. About one in a hundred *is* an angler. About ten in a hundred throw the hatchet better than the fly.

COLONEL PETER HAWKER (1814)

Surf fishing is to saltwater angling what trout fishing is to fresh water. It's a one-man game from start to finish.

VAN CAMPEN HEILNER (C. 1922)

Rainbow trout fishing is as different from brook fishing as prize fighting is from boxing.

ERNEST HEMINGWAY (1920)

Somebody just back of you while you are fishing is as bad as someone looking over your shoulder while you write a letter to your girl.

ERNEST HEMINGWAY (1923)

There is great pleasure in being on the sea, in the unknown wild suddenness of a great fish; in his life and death which he lives for you in an hour while your strength is harnessed to his; and there is satisfaction in conquering this thing which rules the sea it lives in.

ERNEST HEMINGWAY (1936)

As for being Sportsman being Artist, I always fished and shot since I could carry a canepole or a single-barrelled shotgun; not to show off but for great inner pleasure and almost complete satisfaction. Have not been writing as long but get the same pleasure, and you do it alone.

ERNEST HEMINGWAY (1936)

A friend in Texas, to whom I sent a bass-fly and who had never seen a fly before, enthusiastically declared it to be a fish-hook poetized, and thought that a Black bass should take it through a love of the beautiful, if nothing else.

JAMES HENSHALL (1881)

I yield to no one in love and admiration for the brook trout. I was perfectly familiar with it before I ever saw a black bass; but I am not so blinded by prejudice but that I can share that love with the black bass, which for several reasons is destined to become the favorite game-fish of America.

JAMES HENSHALL (1881)

The Black Bass is eminently an American fish. . . . He is plucky, game, brave and unyielding to the last when hooked. . . . I consider him, inch for inch and pound for pound, the gamest fish that swims.

JAMES HENSHALL (1881)

You must lose a fly to catch a trout.

GEORGE HERBERT (1631)

You must remember that there's plenty of salt in the sea to take with the tales your fellow fishermen tell.
JOHN HERSEY (1987)

The ancients wrote of the three ages of man; I propose to write of the three ages of the fisherman.

When he wants to catch all the fish he can.

When he strives to catch the largest fish.

When he studies to catch the most difficult fish he can find, requiring the greatest skill and most refined tackle, caring more for the sport than the fish.
EDWARD R. HEWITT (1948)

She is neither fish nor flesh, nor good red herring.
JOHN HEYWOOD (1546)

He seems to regard angling as an amusement in which to pass the time pleasantly, rather than as a craft to be closely studied.
W. EARL HODGSON (1920)

Where the pools are bright and deep,
   Where the grey trout lies asleep,
Up the river and over the lea,
   That's the way for Billy and me.
    JAMES HOGG (C. 1810)

For you catch your next fish with a piece of the last.
  OLIVER WENDELL HOLMES (C. 1894)

Of beetling rocks that overhang the flood
Where silent anglers cast insidious food
With fraudful care await the finny prize
And sudden lift it quivering to the skies . . .
   HOMER (8TH CENTURY B.C.)

Though my float goes swimmingly on,
My bad luck never seems to diminish;
   It would seem that the bream
   Must be scarce in the stream,
And the chub, though it's chubby, be thinnish!
   THOMAS HOOD (C. 1830)

There were lots of people who committed crimes during the year who would not have done so if they had been fishing, and I assure you that the increase in crime is due to a lack of those qualities of mind and character which impregnate the soul of every fisherman except those who get no bites.

HERBERT HOOVER (1930)

Fishing is a chance to wash one's soul with pure air, with the rush of the brook, or with the shimmer of the sun on the blue water. . . . And it is discipline in the equality of man—for all men are equal before fish.

HERBERT HOOVER (1963)

The political potency of fish is known to Presidents as well as candidates. In modern times all Presidents quickly begin to fish soon after election. I am told that McKinley, Taft, Wilson, and Harding all undertook fishing in a tentative way, but for the common fishes.

HERBERT HOOVER (1963)

Glory be to God for dappled things—
For skies as couple-color as a brinded cow;
For rose-moles all in stipple upon trout that swim.
GERARD MANLEY HOPKINS (1918)

Artificial flie Angling is the most gentil, ingenious, pleasonat and profitable part of the inncoent Recreation of Angling; to the perfect Accomplishment of which, is required, not only good affection and frequent practise, but also diligent Observation and considerable Judgement; especially in the choice of Materials and mixing of colours for flies.

ROBERT HOWLETT (1706)

If he prove a large fish, pull not, but hold your rod still, the butt end outward towards the fish, til you can turn him as one would turn an unruly horse. But if he will run out a stretch, and you cannot follow him, then if the place be clear, throw your rod in after him, and commend all to Fortune, rather than lose hook, line, and fish.

ROBERT HOWLETT (1706)

Fishermen by ones and twos and threes were climbing over the fence, and heading off. . . . About one out of three crossed the fence, peeled out of the line flowing downriver, and headed for the willows.

"Look at them," the old man chided. "They're wearing and carrying the most sophisticated fly-fishing equipment in the world, and they haven't even learned to pee before they put their waders on."

DAVE HUGHES (1982)

As he had often happened to find in perfectly limpid sea water tolerably large animals of strange and various shape of the species medusa, which, out of water, resembled soft crystal, and which thrown back into the water, blended with their surroundings in transparency and color, he drew the conclusion that since living transparencies inhabit the water, other transparencies, equally living, might also inhabit the air.

VICTOR HUGO (C. 1880)

To look into the depths of the sea is to behold the imagination of the Unknown.

VICTOR HUGO (C. 1880)

The reason that all other kinds of fishermen look up to the dry-fly purist is not that he catches more fish than they; on the contrary, it is because he catches fewer. His is the sport in its purest, most impractical, least material form.

WILLIAM HUMPHREY (1978)

Anglers boast of the innocence of their pastime, yet it puts fellow creatures to torture. They pique themselves on their meditative faculties; and yet their only excuse is a want of thought.

LEIGH HUNT (1821)

There is certainly something in angling . . . that seems to produce a gentleness of spirit, and a pure serenity of mind.

WASHINGTON IRVING (C. 1820)

The adventurous life of the angler, amidst our wild scenery, on our vast lakes and rivers, must furnish a striking contrast to the quiet loiterings of the English angler along the Trent or Dove.

WASHINGTON IRVING (C. 1820)

And I think, as I angle for fish,
    In the hope that my hooks will attach 'em,
It's delightfully easy to fish—
    But harder than blazes to catch 'em.
    WALLACE IRWIN (1904)

Of all the fish that swim or swish
    In ocean's deep autocracy,
There's none possess such haughtiness
    As the codfish aristocracy.
    WALLACE IRWIN (1904)

Within the pool's abysmal dun
A salmon eyes the shattered sun:
Salmon and water move as one.
    WILLIAM JEFFREY (C. 1915)

I don't want to ketch no tarpon that weighs half a ton.
And feedin' clams to sheepshead isn't just what I call fun.
Of salmon when it's boiled or baked I'll say that I am fond—
But when I'm after sport I fish for pick'rel in a pond.

NORMAN JEFFRIES (C. 1905)

A slender rod, a silken line, an invisible leader of hairlike fineness, a counterfeit fly cunningly devised of fur and feathers and steel, a surface-feeding trout, the cast, the strike, the net, and another trout goes the way of all flesh.

PRESTON JENNINGS (1935)

Canst thou draw out leviathan with a hook?

JOB 41:1 (C. 325 B.C.)

Simon Peter saith unto them, I go a fishing. They say unto him, we also go with thee. They went forth, and entered into a ship immediately; and that night they caught nothing.

JOHN 21:3 (C. 115)

Fly-fishing may be a very pleasant amusement; but angling, or float-fishing, I can only compare to a stick and a string, with a worm at one end and a fool at the other.
SAMUEL JOHNSON (C. 1730)

Fish dinners will make a man spring like a flea.
THOMAS JORDAN (C. 1670)

Give me the patience to sit calmly by,
While amateurs with veterans gravely vie,
Recounting deeds performed with rod and fly.
Then help me tell the FINAL, CROWNING LIE!
C. J. JUDD (C. 1912)

The fisherman could perhaps be bought for less than the fish.
JUVENAL (C. 100)

Men call Salmon "capricious"; but is not the term a cover for their own ignorance about the habits of the fish and the flies they show them, rather than the truthful representation of facts?

GEORGE KELSON (1895)

Fly fishing is a very gory amusement.

RUDYARD KIPLING (1890)

On the road to Mandalay,
Where the flyin'-fishes play . . .

RUDYARD KIPLING (1892)

The beginner has a long, hard road to travel and he is due for many heartaches and fishless days. But then every trade must be learned through apprenticeship.

JOHN ALDEN KNIGHT (1936)

Not being able to see them does not mean that they are not there; a big brown trout will find a hiding place on a ballroom floor if he has six inches of water in which to swim.

JOHN ALDEN KNIGHT (1936)

Cautious and wily but not shy and timid; pugnacious and game to the core; always ready for an argument and equipped to hold up his end; the black bass is a grand fish any way you look at him.

JOHN ALDEN KNIGHT (1936)

If a little madness be a necessary requisite to obtain the ultimate in the pleasure of angling—then, O Lord, give me insanity!

JOHN ALDEN KNIGHT (1936)

One of the outstanding peculiarities of angling is its inexplicable capacity to inspire almost unanimous disagreement among its followers.

JOHN ALDEN KNIGHT (1936)

I once heard a Presbyterian minister . . . openly declare that if he found it necessary to choose fifty men for a mission which required courage and dependability he would much prefer to make his choice of fifty anglers rather than of fifty Presbyterians.

JOHN ALDEN KNIGHT (1936)

Often, I have been exhausted on trout streams, uncomfortable, wet, cold, briar-scarred, sunburned, mosquito-bitten, but never, with a fly rod in my hand, have I been in a place that was less than beautiful.

CHARLES KURALT (1990)

Even though competition has no place in fly fishing, and should have none, the angler ought to strive always to play a good game. He should practice the tactics of his art with the same zeal as do the followers of competitive sports if he hopes ever to become an expert fly fisherman in the highest sense of that much misused term.

GEORGE LA BRANCHE (1914)

A possum hound, he simply said, is just a coonhound that has failed.

As far as fishing went right then, I knew I was a possum hound.

DANA LAMB (1973)

The waiter he to him doth call,
And gently whispers—"One Fish ball."
The waiter roars it through the hall,
"The guests they start at One Fish ball!"
The guest then says, quite ill at ease,
"A piece of bread, sir, if you please."
The waiter roars it through the hall:
"We don't give bread with one Fish ball!"

GEORGE LANE (1855)

Within the streams, Pausanias saith,
That down Cocytus valley flow,
Girdling the grey domain of Death,
The spectral fishes come and go;
The ghosts of trout flit to and fro.
Persephone, fulfill my wish,
And grant that in the shades below
My ghost may land the ghosts of fish!
ANDREW LANG (C. 1890)

However bad the sport, it keeps you young, or makes you young again, and you need not follow Ponce de Leon to the western wilderness, when, in any river you knew of yore, you can find the fountain of youth.
ANDREW LANG (1891)

On a trout stream only the space near to hand is important. The immediate stretch of river you confront holds enough challenge to eclipse everything beyond its strict boundaries, if just for a little while. The entire world is reduced to a single riffle.
GLENN LAW (1988)

And in mine opinion I could highly commend your orchard, if either through it, or hard by it, there should runne a pleasant River with silver streams; you might sit in your Mount, and angle a speckled Trout or sleighty Eele, or some other dainty fish.

WILLIAM LAWSON (1618)

Trout, as everyone knows who is an angler, never rise after a rain, nor before one; it is impossible to get them to rise in the heat; and any chill in the air keeps them down. The absolutely right day is a still, cloudy day, but even then there are certain kinds of clouds that prevent a rising of the trout. Indeed, I have only to say to one of my expert friends, "Queer, they didn't bite!" and he's off to a good start with an explanation.

STEPHEN LEACOCK (1936)

Calico Jam,
The little Fish swam,
Over the syllabub sea.
EDWARD LEAR (1871)

By making a line of cocoon silk, a hook of a sharp needle, a rod of a branch of bramble or dwarf bamboo, and using a grain of cooked rice for bait, one can catch a whole cartload of fish.

LIEH TZU (4TH CENTURY B.C.)

And the mighty sturgeon, Nahma,
Said to Ugudwash, the sun-fish,
To the bream, with scales of crimson,
"Take the bait of this great boaster,
Break the line of Hiawatha!"

HENRY WADSWORTH LONGFELLOW (1859)

And when they come his deeds to weigh,
   And how he used the talents his,
One trout-scale in the scales he'll lay
(if trout had scales), and t'will outsway
   The wrong side of the balances.

JAMES RUSSELL LOWELL (1866)

Fish and guests in three days are stale.
JOHN LYLY (1579)

All fish are not caught with flies.
JOHN LYLY (1579)

Just as I would not write down, I would not write up. What I was doing, I hoped, with as much skill and invisible artifice as I could muster—as little of the factitious, the posturing as possible—was to report on days afield, and the nature of my relationship to the sport, a relationship that included having, at various times, the keenest possible interest in the minutiae of fly fishing; not using the fancy or occult words, or the Latin, or the names of people and places to impress, but choosing, always, the fullest, most personal way to tell where I'd been. A Trico is a Trico is a Trico; it is not merely a small black fly, nor is it a rose.

I had tried, for more than twenty-five years, to find and to build a language that represented me—something with feeling but not sentimentality, a voice playful but not mannered, not down, not up, not safe, not different just to be different. Some clever populist once wrote to a fishing magazine complaining of the literary references in the essays I wrote—to Yeats, Keats, Kafka, and Chaucer—as if these had been laid on with a trowel, with pretensions. He had deliberately misspelled every other word in his letter, feigning a superior ignorance, to defend something called the common man. But I read Yeats and Keats and Kafka in my twenties, on my own, and they changed my life. I wouldn't think of hiding them. They are as much my friends as Len and Mike and Doug; they are as much a part of my speech as Tricos and 7X tippets. Do we read books to get bland pap or mere information or clever nonsense, or to touch another human being? I want those who read me to touch me, to know me—for better or worse—not some studied mask I might put on. And this is the stew of me: Yeats and PMDs [mayflies], wit that leavens and builds proportion, not sophisticated but (I hope) not dumb, a warm mulch that heats the postmodernist chill. I'd like the stew to be rich enough to catch some of the stillness, complexity, joy, fierce intensity, frustration, practicality, hilarity, fascination, satisfaction that I find in fly fishing. I'd like it to be fun, because fly fishing is fun—not ever so serious and self-conscious that I take it to be either a religion or a way of life, or a source of salvation. I like it passionately but I try to remember what Cezanne once said after a happy day of fishing: he'd had lots of fun, but it "doesn't lead far."

NICK LYONS (1992)

Crotch, Mak, a fish ain't a fact. It's a fish. A whole lot of foolishness c'ud be avoided in this world if folks w'ud keep their facts an' fish separated.

ARTHUR MACDOUGALL (1946)

To tell the truth, if I knew all erbout fishin' fer trout, I w'ud give it up an' tackle sunthin' more int'resting.

ARTHUR MACDOUGALL (1946)

In our family, there was no clear line between religion and fly fishing.

NORMAN MACLEAN (1976)

. . . all good things—trout as well as eternal salvation—come by grace and grace comes by art and art does not come easy.

NORMAN MACLEAN (1976)

Always it was to be called a [fishing] rod. If someone called it a pole, my father looked at him as a sergeant in the United States Marines would look at a recruit who had just called a rifle a gun.

NORMAN MACLEAN (1976)

Eventually, all things merge into one, and a river runs through it. The river was cut by the world's great flood and runs over rocks from the basement of time. On some of the rocks are timeless raindrops. Under the rocks are the words, and some of the words are theirs.

I am haunted by waters.

NORMAN MACLEAN (1976)

The confirmed man of the trout should resolve to get along with wood ticks. Any other procedure will fail because the wood tick is determined to get along with trout fishermen.

GORDON MACQUARRIE (1947)

One of the best things about trout fishing is going back to a familiar place. Then the woods welcome a man. It is not like being alone on a strange river.

GORDON MACQUARRIE (1947)

Of course you still love her—
    You love, without doubt,
But one thing above her,
    And that is a trout.
It's just the old Adam,
    Man back in his groove.
To quiet the madam
    It's easy to prove
In the Bible you read in,
    As all can perceive,
That Adam loved Eden
    Before he loved Eve!

DOUGLAS MALLOCH (C. 1912)

Fish think they're so smart. Just because they get to loll in the water all the time, while the rest of us have to get out when our lips turn blue or our two weeks' holiday runs out, they think they deserve special treatment in everything.

At the dinner table there are special rules for the eating of fish that friendly animals, such as veal and mutton, wouldn't dream of requiring. Take the matter of bones and pit removal. Miss Manners is always telling people the simple rule about removing undesirable material from the mouth: It goes out the way it came in. A bit of chicken bone that went in by fork goes out by fork. . . . But that's not good enough for fish. Fish have to be the exception, and fish bones that go in by fish fork are nevertheless entitled to a return trip by hand. This unwillingness to go along with the crowd does not make fish popular. Some people won't eat them at all because they don't want anything to do with them, and others who, out of kind-heartedness, don't eat agreeable animals, don't mind eating fish, whom they think of as being cold. You might call someone a "cold fish," but you wouldn't call a different sort of person "a hot, passionate fish."

This may be the reason that fish is often served with the head still on. No one would have the gumption to dig into a turkey while its beady eye was staring up from the plate, but a fish head is not

considered to have a reproachful expression, so many people are able to ignore it. They have enough trouble dealing with the body.
MISS MANNERS (JUDITH MARTIN, 1982)

The people are like water and the army is like fish.
MAO TSE-TUNG (1948)

At present, fishermen are chiefly indebted to the fly-makers of Great Britain for copies of the insects alluring to game fish. Their experience extends back for centuries before our time or country even, and until we have studied more thoroughly our own [American] stream-life we do well to abide by many of their conclusions; but there can be no question that in the years to come the differences between the insects of the two countries will be better understood and defined.
MARY ORVIS MARBURY (1892)

. . . in the lexicon of the fly-fishermen, the words rise and hooked connote the successful and desirable climax; landing a fish is purely anticlimax.
VINCENT C. MARINARO (1950)

A skillful Angler ought to be a general scholar, and seen in all the liberal sciences, as a Grammarian, to know how either to write or discourse on his Art in true terms, either without affection or rudeness.

GERVASE MARKHAM (1635)

Now for those seasons which are nought to angle in, there is none worse than in the violent heat of the day, or when the Winds are loudest, Rain heaviest, Snow and Hail extremest; Thunder and lightning are offensive, or any sharp air which flyeth from the East; the places where men use to wash sheep you shall for bear, for the very smell of the wool will chase fish from their haunts. Land floods are enemies to Anglers, so also at the fall of the leaf is the shedding of leaves into the water, and many other such like pollutions.

GERVASE MARKHAM (1635)

The angler must intice, not command his reward, and that which is worthy millions to his contentment, another may buy for a groate in the Market.

GERVASE MARKHAM (1635)

PREFACE TO A BOOK OF FISHHOOKS

This little book of flies and hooks and guts and hackles, which was presented to us by a friend who heard us say we liked to go fishing —we may as well admit at once that it is full of riddles we cannot rede. We know nothing about trout, and have no great ambition to learn. Fishing for trout has too much exertion and bodily effort about it to be attractive. One tramps over rough country and gets one's self wet in cold water, and tangles one's hook in one's hair and ears, and all that sort of thing.

Our idea of fishing is to put all the exertion up to the fish. If they are ambitious we will catch them. If they are not, let them go about their business. If a fish expects to be caught by us he has to look alive. We give him his opportunity, and he must make the most of it.

DON MARQUIS (C. 1925)

The artificial breeding of domestic fish . . . is apparently destined to occupy an extremely conspicuous place in the history of man's efforts to compensate his prodigal waste of the gifts of nature.

GEORGE PERKINS MARSH (1864)

Beware of taking to collect books on angling. You will find yourself become so attached to the fascinating hobby, that you would, if necessary, pawn the shirt off your back to obtain some coveted edition.

R. B. MARSTON (1894)

Can the fish love the fisherman?

MARTIAL (C. A.D. 85)

Ye monsters of the bubbling deep
    Your Maker's praises spout;
Up from the sands ye codlings peep
    And wag your tails about.

COTTON MATHER (C. 1700)

But as for you, that will tarry, and worship the Lord Jesus Christ this Day, I will pray unto Him for you, that you may take Fish till you are weary.

COTTON MATHER (1702)

And he saith unto them, Follow me, and I will make you fishers of men.

MATTHEW 4:19 (C. 75)

For eels and wild ducks, put hooks upon warp or line, about a foot apart, and the same length to each hook; put a gudgeon on one hook, and a piece of lights on the other all the way. The lights will swim, which the ducks will take, and the eels will take the gudgeons; so, when you draw the line out, you will have a duck on one hook and an eel on the other. This you will find to be excellent sport.

JOHN MAYER (C. 1860)

The important thing in putting together an outfit is not to look for a line that will sail across the Missouri or a rod that will toss a lead sinker over the post office, but a modest set of tools designed to baffle a trout lying in plain sight.

A. J. MCCLANE (1965)

Trying to catch fish distinguishes the angler from other walkers in nature, and, as the angler binds himself by arbitrary rules, to catch fish with difficulty is his unique pleasure.

JOHN MCDONALD (1972)

The central impulse of the angler is to engage nature; it is to that end that he observes nature in detail.

JOHN MCDONALD (1972)

Had all the Pens that go salmon fishing devoted themselves to jotting down notes about why the big fish did not gobble a grass-hopper, we should have lost many a page of sunshine, fresh air, and good fellowship, and reaped a crop of fireside Disko troops who thought like the fish.

WILLIAM MCFARLAND (1925)

What is emphatic in angling is made so by the long silences—the unproductive periods.

TOM MCGUANE (1980)

Anglers of experience speculate a good deal about the character of their quarry, doting on the baleful secrecy of brown trout, the countrified insouciance and general funkiness of largemouth bass, or the vaguely Ivy League patina of brook trout and Atlantic salmon.

TOM MCGUANE (1980)

Mr. [Calvin] Coolidge's exploits as a fisherman are well known. One of his favorite angling places was the River Brule. Once a newspaper reporter asked him how many fish approximately were in the Brule, and the President answered that the waters were estimated to contain about 45,000 fish.

"I haven't caught them all yet," he said, "but I've intimidated them."

JOHN MCKEE (1933)

I bet that a person who thought up a lot of quotations related to the outdoor sports could practically achieve, uh, immortality.

PATRICK MCMANUS (1984)

I disengage the lure and let the grayling go, being mindful not to wipe my hands on my shirt. Several days in use, the shirt is approaching filthy, but here among grizzly bears I would prefer to stink of humanity than of fish.

JOHN MCPHEE (1977)

The art of fly fishing may be attained by surrendering our egos to the stream. And when we have done so, we are likely to recapture innocence again, a catch beside which a cartful of trophy trout is insignificant.

FRANK MELE (1988)

In seeing some of the new fishermen on the old riffles, I'm reminded of a friend who told me he's recently taken up golf because he likes the clothes.

JOHN MERWIN (1993)

Fortunately, fishing has almost no public entertainment value, and . . . I hope it will always remain free from the pressure of competition.

JAMES MICHENER (1976)

The high quality of writing devoted to fishing is a tribute to its values.

JAMES MICHENER (1976)

I have tested every recommendation—tried it fresh, flipped from sea to skillet, tried it marinated in everything from chili vinegar and garlic to a pint of Thunderbird wine, soaked in everything from hollandaise sauce to home-brewed gator sweat, even tried barbecuing it under a full moon. Nothing helps. It is always bluefish and it always goes down like shellac and tastes like a beaker of cod oil.

HARRY MIDDLETON (1993)

. . . not everything about fishing is noble and reasonable and sane. . . . Fishing is not an escape from life, but often a deeper immersion into it, all of it, the good and the awful, the joyous and the miserable, the comic, the embarassing, the tragic, and the sorrowful.

HARRY MIDDLETON (1993)

That's what I like about fly fishing—it accommodates the awkward as well as the graceful, the dreamer as well as the technician, the forgetful as well as the precise and meticulous, the ingenue as well as the brute.

HARRY MIDDLETON (1993)

Fly fishers are notorious for not explaining what they are doing to their spouses or to strangers. It is too complicated, they think, or else it is like jazz in Louis Armstrong's paradox: if it has to be explained, it can't be.

M. R. MONTGOMERY (1991)

The Muse has always smiled on anglers . . . while seeking the sources of their bright streams, they find, in some magical way, the holy and secret sources of poetry also, so that when they tell of rivers and water meadows they speak with the tongues of angels; or perhaps there is some similarity about making a cast and making a sentence—both must be accurate, graceful, rhythmical and neat.

JOHN MOORE (C. 1910)

Probably it was in that moment that all the bickerings and back-talk of husbands and wives originated; when Adam called Eve to come and look at his First Fish while it was still silver and vivid in its living colors; and Eve answered she was busy.

CHRISTOPHER MORLEY (C. 1930)

Once in the lobby of the Midland Hotel in Manchester when I happened to be in some public disfavor, a man came up to me, grasped my hand and observed: "Never forget that only dead fish swim with the stream."

MALCOLM MUGGERIDGE (1964)

Yet respectable-looking, even wise-looking people were fixing bits of worms on bent pieces of wire to catch trout. Sport they called it. Should church-goers try to pass the time fishing in baptismal fonts while dull sermons were being preached, the so-called sport might not be so bad; but to play in the Yosemite temple, seeking pleasure in the pain of fishes struggling for their lives, while God himself is preaching his sublimest water and stone sermons!

JOHN MUIR (1911)

All good fishermen stay young until they die, for fishing is the only dream of youth that doth not grow stale with age.

J. W. MULLER (1909)

Isn't a good Angler as good as a good Deacon, anyway?

W. H. H. MURRAY (1891)

Wha'll buy my caller herrin'?
    The're no brought here without brave darin'.
Buy my caller herrin',
    Ye little ken their worth.
Wha'll buy my caller herrin'?
    Oh, you may ca' them vulgar farin',
Wives and mithers maist despairin'
    Ca' them lives o' men.
    LADY CAROLINA NAIRNE (C. 1825)

What an idiot is man to believe that abstaining from flesh, and eating fish, which is so much more delicate and delicious, constitutes fasting.

NAPOLEON I (1817)

No fisherman ever fishes as much as he wants to—this is the first great rule of fishing, and it explains a world of otherwise inexplicable behavior.

GEOFFREY NORMAN (1981)

What impels him to pursue the tarpon—a piscatorial slob with a cheap suit of theatrical armor and a mouth like a vacuum cleaner? Trout, sí! Salmon, sí! You can make fishmeal of all the rest for me.

PAUL O'NEIL (1964)

A bite, hurrah! The length'ning line extends
Above the tugging fish the arch'd rod bends.

OPPIAN (C. 215)

Here's a guy standing in cold water up to his liver throwing the world's most expensive clothesline at trees.

P. J. O'ROURKE (ON FLY FISHING, 1988)

It is not easy to tell one how to cast. The art must be acquired by practice.

CHARLES ORVIS (1883)

Ever let your hook be hanging; where you least believe it, there will be a fish in the stream.

OVID (C. 5)

We fish to ease the pain of a divorce or the death of a beloved; to earn a living; to remember or to forget who we may have been and who we may have loved; or just to get the hell out of some jagged, hectic place and into some other place—slower, prettier.

MARGOT PAGE (1991)

No fish ever gave the alarm in a burning building by barking or played with a ball of yarn on the hearth. The most you can say for the fish is that he has a certain icy composure and austere dignity.

S. J. PERELMAN (1958)

There is much to be said, in a world like ours, for taking the world as you find it and for fishing with a worm.

BLISS PERRY (1904)

What Walton does for us transcends all mechanical devices and all scientific knowledge of the nature and habits of fish. . . . He does not merely furnish a manual of instruction: he teaches a way of life.

BLISS PERRY (1928)

A trout is a fish known mainly by hearsay. It lives on anything not included in a fisherman's equipment.

H. I. PHILLIPS (C. 1925)

And ete the olde fishe, and leve the young,
Though they moore towghe be uppon the tonge.

PIERS OF FULHAM (1420)

Fishing is a perfectible art, in which nevertheless no man is ever perfect.

GIFFORD PINCHOT (1936)

To take out of a place too shallow or too public or too little promising to be fished by others, a fish good fishermen have passed by, still warms the cockles of my heart.

GIFFORD PINCHOT (1936)

If I were asked to give one word of advice to the angler planning to take his family with him on a fishing holiday, I'd give it: Don't.

JOE PISARRO (1966)

Fishing is not an occupation worthy of a man well born or well brought up, because it demands more of address and ruse than force, and is not for young people, like hunting, the occasion of healthy exercise.

PLATO (C. 390 B.C.)

She was used to take delight, with her fair hand
To angle in the Nile, where the glad fish,
As if they knew who 'twas sought to deceive them,
Contended to be taken.

PLUTARCH (DESCRIBING CLEOPATRA, C. 85)

A West Yellowstone worm fisherman inherited a farm from an uncle and decided to raise trout. He went to a hatchery and bought 100 six-inch rainbows, brought them home and dug 100 holes, in which he planted the trout, up to their neck—in soil.

They all soon died, so he bought 100 more trout, this time planting them with their tails in the air. Again, all died. He decided to get some advice on raising trout, so he wrote to Montana Fish & Game.

In reply, Montana Fish & Game stated they would be unable to help until they received a soil sample.

MILFORD STANLEY POLTROON (DAVID BASCOM, 1977)

Fish should be cleaned immediately after catching for best flavor and aroma. Fishermen also smell better if they are bathed from time to time.

MILFORD STANLEY POLTROON (DAVID BASCOM, 1977)

Trout thrive best in water with a high mineral content, while this is the very sort of water that is worst for making Tennessee whiskey. This is why one never finds a trout in a fifth of Jack Daniel's. Or vice versa.

MILFORD STANLEY POLTROON (DAVID BASCOM, 1977)

A great cloud of black flies hung in the air when the feeding started. Where all had been stillness, but moments before, now became the scene of frantic ingestion of food. The slurping, gulpings, slobberings and suckings—like water trying to get through a clogged drain—were clearly audible to all the anglers nearby. And, of course, the frenzied dartings, wild splashings and tearing at the food supply were plainly visible. Then it stopped, as suddenly as it had begun.

The two bait fishermen paid their check and walked out of the West Yellowstone café.

MILFORD STANLEY POLTROON (DAVID BASCOM, 1977)

Our plenteous streams a various race supply;
The bright-ey'd perch, with fins of Tyrian dye,
The silver eel, in shining volumes roll'd,
The yellow carp, in scales bedrop'd with gold,
Swift trouts, diversify'd with crimson stains,
And pykes, the tyrants of the wat'ry plains.
ALEXANDER POPE (C. 1730)

Oh, where'd I catch them? Well, you can't get there from here; it's uphill both ways. And besides, it's a government secret. If I tell you, I'll have to kill you.
CHARLIE POWELL (1994)

The contentment which fills the mind of the angler at the close of his day's sport is one of the chiefest charms in his life.
WILLIAM COWPER PRIME (1873)

Science, art, and magic are all good; a fishing attitude that squeezes out any of them is the worse for it.
DATUS PROPER (1988)

Fishing is hope experienced. . . . Catching a fish is hope affirmed.
PAUL QUINNETT (1994)

We have other fish to fry.
RABELAIS (1552)

He shines and stinks like rotten mackeral by moonlight.
JOHN RANDOLPH (C. 1810)

If there is any one thing that a strong hardy outdoorsman likes more than another, it is to catch a fish on some unusual makeshift tackle. Let a man use a ping-pong ball for a float and catch a fish that way and he becomes insufferable.
JOHN W. "JACK" RANDOLPH (1956)

There must be some kind of equation to express the relation between the use of small dry flies and the use of the truth. There are men alive today who have used them both, probably, but not at the same time.
JOHN W. "JACK" RANDOLPH (1956)

In their old age, rivers—again like men—grow ponderous and portly, spreading out and slowing down, always moving but somehow more reluctant now to go to their destiny. But finally the river flows across the last bar and is swallowed in the sea, quickly lost in all the waters that have gone before.

STEVE RAYMOND (1973)

There is no monopoly on courage. It is the quality of courage found in fish that leads men to fish for them. And it is something of the same quality in man himself that keeps him wading bravely through swift waters even when the hour is late and shadows are closing in around him.

STEVE RAYMOND (1973)

Compare the strong bull of Bashan with a saltwater smelt. Who doubts the superiority of the bull? Yet, if you drop them both into the Atlantic ocean, I will take my chances with the smelt.

THOMAS BRACKETT REED (1894)

No high ambition may I claim—
I angle not for lordly game
Of trout, or bass, a wary bream—
A black perch reaches the extreme
Of my desires; and goggle-eyes
Are not a thing that I despise;
A sunfish, or a chub or cat—
A silver-side—yea, even that!
JAMES WHITCOMB RILEY (C. 1900)

[Saltwater fly fishing] is only for the strong man with a hard stomach. It is like sex after lunch!
CHARLES RITZ (C. 1974)

For bottom fishing is no mere avocation, rationalization, or even technique. It is a distinctive way of looking at the world.
LOUIS RUBIN (1983)

No human being, however great, or powerful, was ever so free as a fish.

JOHN RUSKIN (C. 1880)

A bass is a good soldier. He always carries the fight to the enemy.

CLARENCE SCHOENFIELD (1947)

Many trout fishermen are not too much interested by trout-stream insects. They merely want to get away for a few hours on some stream and catch a few fish. Too often, a few fish is exactly what they catch with such a haphazard approach to trout fishing.

ERNEST SCHWIEBERT (1955)

The remarkable literature and tradition of fishing for trout is unmatched by that of any other sport. From its treasury we can draw a single conclusion: anglers are thoughtful men and angling is a contemplative art, and many anglers have been the kind of men who have placed their thoughts and experiences on paper to share them with others. From their books has come literature, and from the literature of fly-fishing have come its legends. . . .

Many have written of their sport in language as lithe and bright-colored as the fish themselves, and for this we are grateful. Through their books, we can return through time and relive their experiences, seeking the source of our own fascination in fly-fishing with the legendary authors themselves as guides to the best water.

ERNEST SCHWIEBERT (1961)

Technical words and phrases have crept out to fuddle fishing, and the simplicity the small boy and Izaak Walton imparted to the sport is becoming burdened with complexity.

JACK DENTON SCOTT (1956)

And lightly on the dimpling eddy fling
The hypocritic fly's unruffled wing.
THOMAS SCOTT (1758)

'Tis blithe the mimic fly to lead,
When to the hook the salmon springs
And the line whistles through the rings.
SIR WALTER SCOTT (1822)

Charlie Brown tells us that happiness is a warm puppy. To this
reporter, happiness is a cold trout.
   ERIC SEVAREID (C. 1980)

I am, out of the ladies' company, like a fish out of the water.
   THOMAS SHADWELL (1679)

Bait the hook well: this fish will bite.
   WILLIAM SHAKESPEARE (1598)

         The pleasant'st angling is to see the fish
         Cut with her golden oars the silver stream,
         And greedily devour the treacherous bait.
            WILLIAM SHAKESPEARE (1598)

A man may fish with the worm that hath eat of a king, and eat of
the fish that hath fed of that worm.
   WILLIAM SHAKESPEARE (1600)

Now, who can solve my problem,
And grant my lifelong wish,
Are fishermen all big liars?
Or do only liars fish?
THEODORE SHARP (C. 1890)

He cannot allow the calling of Peter, James, and John from their boats to pass without a comic miraculous overdraft of fishes, with the net sinking the boats and provoking Peter to exclaim, Depart from me; for I am a sinful man, O Lord, which should probably be translated, I want no more of your miracles; natural fishing is good enough for my boats.

GEORGE BERNARD SHAW (1912)

Near the ford is the choicest spot for luncheon that Nature ever devised. Five big trees, chestnut, elm, ash, oak, and beech, there combine to ward off the sun, and then the stream, always in the shade, babbles round three corners with the impetuousness of a mountain brook. With a brace in the creel, or without it, an angler could never fail in that spot of a divine content. Hard-boiled eggs, a crisp lettuce, bread and butter, and a bottle of amber ale a-cool in the water at his feet—what could appetite want better in so smiling a corner of the world?

HUGH SHERINGHAM (1920)

Let the Purist rejoice in the fly that he dries,
And look down on my practice with hauteur,
    But for me the surprise
    Of the flash of the rise,
The rosy-brown wink under water.

G. E. M. SKUES (1921)

"Then do you mean that I have got to go on catching these damned two-and-a-half pounders at this corner for ever and ever?"

The keeper nodded.

"Hell!" said Mr. Castwell.

"Yes," said his keeper.

G. E. M. SKUES (1932)

Let not the meanness of the word *fish* distaste you, for it will afford as good gold as the mines of Guiana or Potosi.

CAPTAIN JOHN SMITH (C. 1615)

And what sport doth yeild a more pleasing content, and less hurt and change than angling with a hook!

CAPTAIN JOHN SMITH (1616)

When you were a tadpole, and I was a fish,
  In the Palaeozoic time,
And side by side in the ebbing tide
  We sprawled through the ooze and slime.

LANGDON SMITH (1895)

Trout are good to eat, but not that good. Not good enough to justify the torture of pursuing them on opening day.

WALTER W. "RED" SMITH (1963)

Now comes April when intelligent worms go underground because, with the trout season approaching, there is danger of being plucked away from home and loved ones, skewered on a hook and flung into the bitter numbing cold of a mountain brook. This is bad for worms.

WALTER W. "RED" SMITH (1963)

A fish story backed by visual evidence is something you don't run into every day.

WALTER W. "RED" SMITH (1963)

Mere wishes for fishes aren't edible dishes.

JULIAN SNOW (C. 1925)

Fishing is a means of meditating for me. Twirling the hook around and sending it out into the world, my thoughts go out into the world with the hook. I place my sadness on the hook and let the weights pull it down into the deep parts of the lake.

SABRINA SOJOURNER (1991)

> What Fury, say, artificer of ill,
> Arm'd thee, O Xiphias, with thy pointed bill?
> *SOPHOCLES (ON SWORDFISH, C. 450 B.C.)*

From the eels they formed their food in chief,
And eels were called the "Derryfield Beef!"
And the marks of eels were so plain to trace,
That the children looked like eels in the face;
And before they walked—it is well confirmed,
That the children never crept but squirmed.
  WILLIAM STARK (1856)

All Americans believe that they are born fishermen. For a man to admit a distaste for fishing would be like denouncing mother-love and hating moonlight.
  JOHN STEINBECK (1954)

A woman without a man is like a fish without a bicycle.
  GLORIA STEINEM (ATTRIBUTED, C. 1978)

I do not care for your stalwart fellows in india-rubber stockings breasting up mountain torrents with a salmon rod; but I do dearly love the class of man who plies his unfruitful art, forever and a day, by still and depopulated waters.
  ROBERT LOUIS STEVENSON (C. 1880)

I have witnessed enough incidents when men have had their eyes wiped by mere women to wonder whether the Big Fisherman in the Sky looks upon the female of the species with an especially kindly eye.

DOUGLAS SUTHERLAND (1982)

They say fish should swim thrice . . . first it should swim in the sea (do you mind me?), then it should swim in butter, and at last, sirrah, it should swim in good claret.

JONATHAN SWIFT (1738)

The curious thing about fishing is you never want to go home. If you catch anything, you can't stop. If you don't catch anything, you hate to leave in case something might bite.

GLADYS TABER (1941)

Though a man eats fish till his guts crack, yet if he eat no flesh he fasts.

JOHN TAYLOR (1630)

I wind about, and in and out,
  With here a blossom sailing,
And here and there a lusty trout,
  And here and there a grayling.
   ALFRED TENNYSON (C. 1850)

The Artful Angler baits his Hook,
And throws it gently in the Brook;
Which the Fish view with greedy Eyes,
And soon are taken by Surprize.
   ISAIAH THOMAS (1787)

In the breast of every fisherman lurks the heart of a savage, when with great satisfaction he catches and kills his fish. It is only when he enters the kitchen, with its long shelf of cookbooks, that he becomes a civilized being.
 LESLIE THOMPSON (1955)

Who hears the fishes when they cry?
 HENRY DAVID THOREAU (1849)

Time is but the stream I go a-fishing in. I drink at it; but while I drink I see the sandy bottom and detect how shallow it is. Its thin current slides away, but eternity remains. I would drink deeper; fish in the sky, where the bottom is pebbly with stars.

HENRY DAVID THOREAU (1854)

Some circumstantial evidence is very strong, as when you find a trout in the milk.

HENRY DAVID THOREAU (1854)

Fly fishing twists fate like a dream and together with wildness, makes anything possible.

AILM TRAVLER (1991)

The purpose of fishing is to catch fish. You hear a lot of poetic falderal about the beauties of nature and the joys of a day in the open. But if I weren't primarily interested in filling my creel, or even in catching fish and turning them loose—which I frequently do—I would be spooking around through the woods with a pair of binoculars and a bird book.

TED TRUEBLOOD (1949)

Tarpon fishing by night is exciting work, somewhat too exciting for many people.

J. TURNER-TURNER (1902)

There is no use in your walking five miles to fish when you can depend on being just as unsuccessful near home.

MARK TWAIN (SAMUEL LANGHORNE CLEMENS, 1875)

The nice people don't come to the Adirondacks to fish; they come to talk about the fishing twenty years ago.

HENRY VAN DYKE (1890)

There is nothing that attracts human nature more powerfully than the sport of tempting the unknown with a fishing line.

HENRY VAN DYKE (1899)

Fish take all sorts of baits most eagerly and freely, and with the least suspicion or bogling, when you present the same unto them in such order and manner as Nature affords them, or as themselves ordinarily gather them.

ROBERT VENABLES (1662)

All is grist for the fisherman's mill. In fact, the amount of Machiavellian subtlety and guile wrapped up in his person is faintly horrifying to contemplate; he is far more devious than Gromyko. Always lusting after new places to fish, he will unblushingly pick the brain of the local game warden . . . or, having heard a vague rumor that the janitor at City Hall has caught a beautiful mess, descend guilefully upon the village to sniff the air for clues.

JOHN VOELKER (ROBERT TRAVER, 1964)

To paraphrase a deceased patriot, I regret that I have but one life to give to my fishing.

JOHN VOELKER (ROBERT TRAVER, 1964)

Chasing trout is no less wearing and barely less complicated than chasing women.

JOHN VOELKER (ROBERT TRAVER, 1964)

Watching a fisherman preparing for his trout devotionals is like watching a tensed percussionist hanging interminably poised over a tiny triangle merely to smite it a single whack. Both performances are to the uninitiated much ado about nothing; both performers devote far too mighty preparations to far too minuscule results. Obviously, this is the pursuit of madmen.

JOHN VOELKER (ROBERT TRAVER, 1964)

TESTAMENT OF A FISHERMAN

I fish because I love to; because I love the environs where trout are found, which are invariably beautiful, and hate the environs where crowds of people are found, which are invariably ugly; because of all the television commercials, cocktail parties, and assorted social posturing I thus escape; because, in a world where most men seem to spend their lives doing things they hate, my fishing is at once an endless source of delight and an act of small rebellion; because trout do not lie or cheat and cannot be bought or bribed or impressed by power, but respond only to quietude and humility and endless patience; because I suspect that men are going along this way for the last time and I for one don't want to waste the trip; because mercifully there are no telephones on trout waters; because only in the woods can I find solitude without loneliness; because bourbon out of an old tin cup always tastes better out there; because maybe one day I will catch a mermaid; and, finally, not because I regard fishing as being so terribly important but because I suspect that so many of the other concerns of men are equally unimportant and not nearly so much fun.

JOHN VOELKER (ROBERT TRAVER, 1974)

Fly fishing is such great fun, I have often felt, that it really ought to be done in bed.

JOHN VOELKER (ROBERT TRAVER, 1974)

I know of no sport so ridden with taboos, so gangrenous with snobbery, so reeking with cant, as trout fishing.

HOWARD WALDEN (1972)

The fact that Smith and Jones both fish is no more a sign of fundamental kinship between them, no more an earnest of sympathetically beating hearts than is a common liking for turnips.

HOWARD WALDEN (1972)

With whatever lure a man fishes, if he is a plugger he will plug and if he is a skipper he will skip. This matter of tempo is a matter of temperament.

HOWARD WALDEN (1972)

Angling is somewhat like poetry, men are to be born so.

IZAAK WALTON (1653)

I have laid aside business, and gone a-fishing.

IZAAK WALTON (1653)

Angling may be said to be so like the mathematics that it can never be fully learnt.

IZAAK WALTON (1653)

As no man is born an artist, so no man is born an angler.
IZAAK WALTON (1653)

Doubt not but angling will prove to be so pleasant that it will prove to be, like virtue, a reward to itself.
IZAAK WALTON (1653)

This dish of meat is too good for any but anglers, or very honest men.
IZAAK WALTON (1653)

Let the blessing of Saint Peter's Master be upon all that are lovers of virtue, and dare trust in his Providence, and be quiet and go a-angling.
IZAAK WALTON (1653)

I am, Sir, a brother of the Angle.
IZAAK WALTON (1653)

Thus use your frog. . . . Put your hook through his mouth, and out at his gills . . . and then with a fine needle and silk sew the upper part of his leg, with only one stitch, to the arming-wire of your hook; or tie the frog's leg, above the upper joint, to the armed-wire; and in so doing use him as though you loved him.

IZAAK WALTON (1653)

We may say of angling, as Dr. Boteler [Dr. William Butler] said of strawberries: "Doubtless God could have made a better berry, but doubtless God never did"; and so, if I might be judge, God never did make a more calm, quiet, innocent recreation than angling.

IZAAK WALTON (1655)

Even today, some Maine residents scorn bass as tourist fish.

Oh, bass are all right, I guess, a resort owner told me in 1970. There's a man over in Portland who eats the damned things!

CHARLES WATERMAN (1981)

Trout are mysterious. They're quiet and graceful, the oak trees of the fish forest. Mackeral, on the other hand, are noisy fish. They fight like hell. . . . Between the two lie bass, who are middle-of-the-road fish, noncontroversial. . . . I have never met a sturgeon, but I have a hunch that they are downright intellectual (perhaps a bit dark and Russian, too). Salmon are, without a doubt, the most intelligent of fish; they also have an excellent sense of humor.

KATHARINE WEBER (1991)

The day was fine—not another hook in the brook.

DANIEL WEBSTER (C. 1835)

Poor Izaak Walton! Little did he think, when moving along by the banks of the rivers and brooks of Staffordshire, with his cumbrous equipments, that any unworthy disciple of his would ever be so gorgeously fitted out, with all that art and taste can accomplish for the pursuit of his favorite sport!

DANIEL WEBSTER (1847)

"Turbot, Sir," said the waiter, placing before me two fishbones, two eyeballs, and a bit of black mackintosh.

THOMAS WELBY (1932)

My favorite time on the water will continue to be dusk. Not day, not night, but the peaceful edge of beauty in-between.

W. D. WETHERELL (1984)

If I try to come up with an influence that was behind me as I wrote, it would be Kafka—Kafka as a fly fisherman in a long, black coat, casting shyly in some Prague trickle, fishing for the absurd the way other men fish for trout.

W. D. WETHERELL (1984)

These are bass lures; is there anything more typically American in proud illiteracy and cartoon rhythm than their names? River Runt, Bugeye, Cop-e-cat, Flutterchuck, Hawg Frawg, Krocodile, Lusox, Sputterbug, Kweet Special, Augertail, Bopper Popper . . . they're all here, with a flash and energy that are as aural as sound.

W. D. WETHERELL (1984)

A trout killed with a fly is a jewel of price,
But a trout poached with a worm is like throwing cogged dice.

J. P. WHEELDON (1894)

Worms I hate, and never use 'em;
And, kindly friends, ne'er abuse 'em.
J. P. WHEELDON (1894)

A man who has spent much time and money in dreary restaurants moodily chewing filet of sole on the special luncheon is bound to become unmanageable when he discovers that he can produce the main fish course directly at the edge of his own pasture, by a bit of trickery on a fine morning.
E. B. WHITE (1944)

The fisherman fishes as the urchin eats a cream bun—from lust.
T. H. WHITE (1936)

FISHING

Maybe this is fun, sitting in the sun,
  With a book and parasol, as my Angler wishes,
While he dips his line in the ocean brine,
  Under the impression that his bait will catch the fishes.

'Tis romantic, yes, but I must confess
    Thoughts of shady rooms at home somehow seem more
inviting.
But I dare not move—"Quiet, there, my love!"
    Says my Angler, "for I think a monster fish is biting."

"Any luck?" I gently ask of the angler at his task,
    "There's something pulling at my line," he says; "I've almost
caught it."
But when, with blistered face, we our homeward steps retrace,
    We take the little basket just as empty as we brought it.
    ELIA WHEELER WILCOX (C. 1910)

Enjoy the stream, O harmless fish;
And when an angler for his dish,
Through gluttony's vile sin,
Attempts, a wretch, to pull thee out,
God give thee strength, O gentle trout,
To pull the raskall in!
    JOHN WOLCOT (C. 1790)

I have the awful suspicion that [Walton's] *The Compleat Angler*'s stilted prose was contrived and patterned after an earlier blueprint, then tinkered by a herd of stuffy editors down through the centuries. I'll bet Venator really said to Piscator—"For God's sake, Ike, pass that bottle!"

FRANK WOOLNER (1977)

While Flowing rivers yield a blameless sport
Shall live the name of Walton: Sage benign!
Whose pen, the mysteries of rod and line
Unfolding, did not fruitlessly exhort.

WILLIAM WORDSWORTH (C. 1825)

It's better to be the fisherman than the rower.

JOAN SALVATO WULFF (1987)

Yes, this sport fits me—physically, mentally, psychologically. Why do I love trout? For the same reasons men do.

JOAN SALVATO WULFF (1991)

A gamefish is too valuable to be caught only once.
LEE WULFF (1938)

Fly casting, like many other things, is a matter of still and timing —of easy rhythm rather than power. Such things can be enjoyed all through life and perhaps most of all in the more relaxed years of age. Paddle easily. Climb slowly. Choose the right places from the experience of other days, and enjoy the view to the fullest.
LEE WULFF (1983)

The expert angler isn't necessarily a guy who always does the right thing at the right second. But one thing he necessarily is, and that's a fishing man!
PHILIP WYLIE (C. 1950)

THE FISHERMAN

Although I can see him still,
The freckled man who goes
To a grey place on a hill

In grey Connemara clothes
At dawn to cast his flies,
It's long since I began
To call up to the eyes
This wise and simple man.
All day I'd looked in the face
What I had hoped 'twould be
To write for my own race
And the reality;
The living men that I hate,
The dead man that I loved,
The craven man in his seat,
The insolent unreproved,
And no knave brought to book
Who has won a drunken cheer,
The witty man and his joke
Aimed at the commonest ear,
The clever man who cries
The catch-cries of the clown,
The beating down of the wise
And great Art beaten down.

Maybe a twelvemonth since
Suddenly I began,

In scorn of this audience,
Imagining a man,
And his sun-freckled face,
And grey Connemara cloth,
Climbing up to a place
Where stone is dark under froth,
And the down-turn of his wrist
When the flies drop in the stream;
A man who does not exist,
A man who is but a dream;
And cried, "Before I am old
I shall have written him one
Poem maybe as cold
And passionate as the dawn."
WILLIAM BUTLER YEATS (1919)

Angling: incessant expectation, and perpetual disappointment.
ARTHUR YOUNG (1787)

In keeping with White House guidelines, I plan to limit the increase in the number of fish I catch this season to no greater than seven percent. I once calculated the cost of the various support services, equipment, and apparel required to catch a fish, and the total came out somewhere between the costs of operating a Strategic Air Command bomber and a small nuclear energy plant (not including safety measures in the latter, which seem to be optional).

The figures were based on the number of fish caught at the height of my skills, a frenzied peak of activity that spanned some three hours during a prolonged mayfly hatch on Wisconsin's Wolf River in 1967. I allowed for inflation in my calculations—inflation of prices, not, of course, of the number of fish taken.

DONALD ZAHNER (1979)

Fishermen are born honest, but they get over it.

ED ZERN (1945)

Many fishermen use flies instead of worms. They think it is more hoity-toity. If worms cost two bits apiece, and you could dig Royal Coachmen and Parmachenee Belles out of the manure pile, they would think differently. This is called human nature.

ED ZERN (1945)

Ah, happy barefoot youth with bent-pin hook,
    As innocent as saints long dead or latter-day,
Seeking the wily trout in fern-rimmed brook,
    You got Monday, Tuesday, Wednesday, Thursday and
    Friday to splash around in this water, you little hick;
    Why can't you let me fish it in peace on Saturday?
    ED ZERN (1946)

I get all the truth I need in the newspaper every morning, and every chance I get I go fishing, or swap stories with fishermen, to get the taste of it out of my mouth.
    ED ZERN (1977)

Acknowledgments

Thanks to Rick Balkin, my literary agent, whose fine idea this was, and also to Nick Lyons and Darrel Martin for their comments. Friends, indeed.

Thanks also to Jon Matthewson, American Museum of Fly Fishing registrar, for his considerable help in locating sources and for his keen wit.

While this book evolved through countless bits of paper, it also evolved electronically. The following were helpful in responding through global cyberspace to inquiries as to sources that I made among fishermen on the internet: David Engerbretson, Jon Hazen, Charlie Powell, Richard Caccavale, Bill Cass, Chris Holland-Tuve, Conrad Black, and Danny Walls.

My family continues to tolerate with good humor this writer's distractions and the general turbulence of a work in progress, so thanks again to Martha, Emily, Jason, and Sam Merwin. Tonight we'll have supper together, for once.

Tight lines to all, written and otherwise.